Endorsements for the Church Questions Series

"Christians are pressed by very real questions. How does Scripture structure a church, order worship, organize ministry, and define biblical leadership? Those are just examples of the questions that are answered clearly, carefully, and winsomely in this new series from 9Marks. I am so thankful for this ministry and for its incredibly healthy and hopeful influence in so many faithful churches. I eagerly commend this series."

R. Albert Mohler Jr., President, The Southern Baptist Theological Seminary

"Sincere questions deserve thoughtful answers. If you're not sure where to start in answering these questions, let this series serve as a diving board into the pool. These minibooks are winsomely to-the-point and great to read together with one friend or one hundred friends."

Gloria Furman, author, *Missional Motherhood* and *The Pastor's Wife*

"As a pastor, I get asked lots of questions. I'm approached by unbelievers seeking to understand the gospel, new believers unsure about next steps, and maturing believers wanting help answering questions from their Christian family, friends, neighbors, or coworkers. It's in these moments that I wish I had a book to give them that was brief, answered their questions, and pointed them in the right direction for further study. Church Questions is a series that provides just that. Each booklet tackles one question in a biblical, brief, and practical manner. The series may be called Church Questions, but it could be called 'Church Answers.' I intend to pick these up by the dozens and give them away regularly. You should too."

Juan R. Sanchez, Senior Pastor, High Pointe Baptist Church, Austin, Texas

"Where can we Christians find reliable answers to our common questions about life together at church—without having to plow through long, expensive books? The Church Questions booklets meet our need with answers that are biblical, thoughtful, and practical. For pastors, this series will prove a trustworthy resource for guiding church members toward deeper wisdom and stronger unity."

Ray Ortlund, President, Renewal Ministries

How Do I Disciple Others?

Church Questions

Can Women Be Pastors?, Greg Gilbert
Does It Matter What I Believe?, Samuel James
Does the Gospel Promise Health and Prosperity?, Sean DeMars
Does the Old Testament Really Point to Jesus?, David M. King
How Can I Be Sure I'm Saved?, Jeremy Pierre
How Can I Begin to Teach the Bible?, David Helm
How Can I Encourage My Pastors?, Carmyn Zamora
How Can I Get More Out of My Bible Reading?, Jeremy Kimble
How Can I Grow in Hospitality?, Keri Folmar
How Can I Love Church Members with Different Politics?, Jonathan Leeman and Andy Naselli
How Can I Make the Most of Sunday Services?, Erin Wheeler
How Can I Serve My Church?, Matthew Emadi
How Can Women Thrive in the Local Church?, Keri Folmar
How Do I Disciple Others?, J. Garret Kell
How Do I Fight Sin and Temptation?, J. Garret Kell
How Do I Get Started in Evangelism?, Mack Stiles
Is God Really Sovereign?, Conrad Mbewe
Is Hell Real?, Dane Ortlund
Should I Be a Missionary?, Andy Johnson
What Do Deacons Do?, Juan Sanchez
What If I'm Discouraged in My Evangelism?, Isaac Adams
What If I've been Hurt by My Church?, Daniel P. Miller
What Is a Church?, Matthew Emadi
What Is the Church's Mission?, Jonathan Leeman
What Should I Do Now That I'm a Christian?, Sam Emadi
What Should I Look for in a Church?, Alex Duke
Who's in Charge of the Church?, Sam Emadi
Why Should I Be Baptized?, Bobby Jamieson
Why Should I Give to My Church?, Jamie Dunlop
Why Should I Join a Church?, Mark Dever

How Do I Disciple Others?

J. Garret Kell

WHEATON, ILLINOIS

How Do I Disciple Others?

© 2025 by 9Marks

Published by Crossway
    1300 Crescent Street
    Wheaton, Illinois 60187

All rights reserved. No part of this publication may be reproduced, stored in a retrieval system, or transmitted in any form by any means, electronic, mechanical, photocopy, recording, or otherwise, without the prior permission of the publisher, except as provided for by USA copyright law. Crossway® is a registered trademark in the United States of America.

Cover image and design: Jordan Singer

First printing 2025

Printed in the United States of America

Scripture quotations are from the ESV® Bible (The Holy Bible, English Standard Version®), © 2001 by Crossway, a publishing ministry of Good News Publishers. Used by permission. All rights reserved. The ESV text may not be quoted in any publication made available to the public by a Creative Commons license. The ESV may not be translated in whole or in part into any other language.

All emphases in Scripture quotations have been added by the author.

Trade paperback ISBN: 978-1-4335-9609-4
ePub ISBN: 978-1-4335-9611-7
PDF ISBN: 978-1-4335-9610-0

Library of Congress Cataloging-in-Publication Data

Names: Kell, J. Garrett, author.
Title: How do I disciple others? / J. Garrett Kell.
Description: Wheaton, Illinois : Crossway, 2025. | Series: Church questions | Includes bibliographical references and index.
Identifiers: LCCN 2024018891 (print) | LCCN 2024018892 (ebook) | ISBN 9781433596094 (trade paperback) | ISBN 9781433596100 (pdf) | ISBN 9781433596117 (epub)
Subjects: LCSH: Discipling (Christianity) | Spiritual formation.
Classification: LCC BV4520 .K36 2025 (print) | LCC BV4520 (ebook) | DDC 248.4—dc23/eng/20240711
LC record available at https://lccn.loc.gov/2024018891
LC ebook record available at https://lccn.loc.gov/2024018892

Crossway is a publishing ministry of Good News Publishers.

BP		34	33	32	31	30	29	28	27	26	25
15	14	13	12	11	10	9	8	7	6	5	4	3	2	1

Therefore encourage one another
and build one another up,
just as you are doing.

1 Thessalonians 5:11

I'd never felt more helpless in my life.

The nurse escorted me and my wife to our car following the birth of our first child. She ensured our car seat was properly installed and exclaimed through a smile, "See you later!" As she walked away, it hit me—I had no idea what I was doing. I'd never been around babies before, and now I was supposed to raise one!

Today, we have six children. I've learned a lot, but I'm still figuring out how to parent.

Discipling can feel a lot like parenting. We want to help people follow Jesus more faithfully, but we don't always know how. We're typically a few steps ahead of the person we're helping, but we're keenly aware that our lives are still messy. We can imagine a million reasons why God shouldn't use us.

Yet God delights to work in and through imperfect, weak people. Others learn to pray as we grow in our own prayer lives. As we seek counsel from God's word, we model how others ought to mine its pages for spiritual treasures. As we confess our sins and lean on Jesus for his forgiving grace, others learn how to do the same. Discipling is not a mission for perfected Christians; it's an opportunity to say to others, "Come and see the perfect one, Jesus, who will supply our every need" (see John 1:46).

This little book is intended to help you help others follow Jesus. It will give you practical help to obey Jesus's command to "make disciples of all nations" (Matt. 28:19).

To begin, let's answer two questions: *What is a disciple?* and *What is discipling?*

What Is a Disciple?

Most simply, a disciple is a follower.[1] Disciples follow, learn from, and imitate someone.

Christians are disciples of Jesus. He left us an example we should follow (1 Pet. 2:21). Jesus calls us to be his disciples in passages like Luke 9:23–26:

> If anyone would come after me, let him deny himself and take up his cross daily and follow me. For whoever would save his life will lose it, but whoever loses his life for my sake will save it. For what does it profit a man if he gains the whole world and loses or forfeits himself? For whoever is ashamed of me and of my words, of him will the Son of Man be ashamed when he comes in his glory and the glory of the Father and of the holy angels.

Jesus's disciples have repented of sin, forsaken the world, and committed their lives to follow him by faith. Jesus's disciples deny their sinful desires through the power of the Holy Spirit to please their Lord. Jesus's disciples daily lay down their lives for his glory. Jesus's disciples know a day of judgment is coming and strive to live every moment in light of it.

When Jesus calls people to be his disciples, he isn't simply calling them to join a club. He's calling them to turn from their sin and love him every day until they see him face-to-face. Being a disciple of Jesus isn't a one-time decision—it's an ongoing relationship. Each day, we draw upon his grace and strive to live in obedience to him.

What Is Discipling?

Forty days after Jesus rose from the dead, he assembled his disciples and gave them this commission:

> All authority in heaven and on earth has been given to me. Go therefore and make disciples of all nations, baptizing them in the name of the Father and of the Son and of the Holy Spirit, teaching them to observe all that I have commanded you. And behold, I am with you always, to the end of the age. (Matt. 28:18–20)

Jesus instructs his disciples that wherever they go, their primary job is to make disciples. This means every relationship we have should be flavored with either evangelism or discipling. These are the two aspects of "making disciples" in the Great Commission.

First, we make disciples by calling people who don't follow Jesus to follow him. This is called evangelism. We proclaim the good news that Jesus died for sinners like us and that three days later he rose from the dead. We assure people that if they turn away from their sin and believe in him, he will forgive all their sins and reconcile them to God. If they respond rightly, they become Jesus's disciples.

Second, we make disciples by helping people who already know Jesus grow in their relationships with him. We purposefully do spiritual good to them. We help them obey everything Jesus commanded (Matt. 28:20). We help people obey Jesus with their words, their work, their time, their money, their identities, their sexuality, and everything else you can think of. Jesus is the Lord over our whole lives, and everything we do should be aimed at pleasing him (2 Cor. 5:9; Eph. 5:10; Col. 1:10; 1 John 3:22). That's the work of *discipling*.

Why Should I Disciple?

Before we consider how to disciple others, let's consider a few reasons Scripture gives for why we should disciple others.

To Obey God

Discipling is not an elective in the Christian life; it's a required course (Matt. 28:18–20). My friend Mark Dever often says, "If you say you're following Jesus but aren't helping others follow Jesus, I don't know what you mean when you say you're following Jesus." That statement isn't meant to shame us but to sober us. Are you obeying Jesus by helping others follow him? If not, what's stopping you? Remember, Jesus promises to supply everything you need to do what he has called you to do. He gives us his presence (Matt. 28:20), his power (Acts 1:8), his help (John 15:5), and his joy (John 15:11).

To Edify Others

First Thessalonians 5:11 summarizes the goal of discipling: "Encourage one another and build one another up." God's Spirit empowers us to help one another progress in spiritual maturity so that we are strong and stable in God's love (Eph. 4:12–16).

Hannah was young in her faith. She loved Jesus but was easily distracted by movies and social media.[2] Abby, a slightly older sister in Christ in the same small group, befriended Hannah and invited Hannah into her life. Over the course of a year, they prayed together, shared struggles, and mined the Scriptures for God's promises. Hannah's appetite for mindless entertainment faded and her love for God's word deepened. Abby's intentional love and instruction gave Hannah an example of heavenly mindedness that was lovely and inspiring. Our discipling relationships should be marked by the same kind of intentional edification.

As we build up individual believers, we strengthen the body of Christ in our local church. A church full of Abby- and Hannah-like believers will radiate the glory of Christ in a unique way. Their singing will be more robust, their encouragement will be more vibrant, and their love will be made resilient. This love magnifies Jesus and makes a compelling argument for the world that Jesus is indeed the Son of God (John 13:34–35; 17:23).

To Grow Personally

Discipling often includes a mature believer investing in a less mature one. But mature believers learn from younger believers too (Rom. 1:11–12). For instance, Kevin was a faithful brother in his late sixties who spent his retirement teaching young men how to walk with Jesus. During one breakfast meeting, a young man hesitated to comment on a passage they were studying. The young man confessed that he didn't feel like he could offer anything helpful. Kevin looked him in the eyes and said, "The same Holy Spirit who lives in me, lives in you. I need you as much as you need me." Kevin knew that as he invested in younger believers, God would use their zeal, insights, and questions to help him grow in spiritual maturity. We disciple others because as we help others grow, God grows us.

Am I Ready to Disciple?

Discipling someone may feel daunting. If you're like me, you can think of many reasons why God shouldn't use you. But Scripture often reminds us that God specializes in working through people who don't have it all together.

Are you ready to disciple someone? It depends on whether you have faith, fruit, and failures.

Do You Have Faith?

When Jesus called Andrew and Peter to be his disciples, he said, "Follow me, and I will make you fishers of men" (Matt. 4:19). Before anyone can become a fisher of men, they must be a follower of Jesus. How could we help others know Jesus if we don't know him ourselves?

Discipling flows from our own personal devotion to Jesus (1 Cor. 11:1). If we neglect our own repentance and faith, we will lead people into great spiritual harm. Consider Jesus's warnings to the religious leaders of his day, "Woe to you, scribes and Pharisees, hypocrites! For you travel across sea and land to make a single proselyte, and when he becomes a proselyte, you make him twice as much a child of hell as yourselves" (Matt. 23:15). If you're going to help others walk in a way that honors God, you must first have saving faith in Jesus so that you'll lead them toward heaven not hell.

Do You Have Fruit?

Discipling isn't merely an intellectual enterprise of passing information to others. We need to share with others a faith that can be observed and imitated. As the author of Hebrews exhorted his readers, "Remember your leaders, those who spoke to you the word of God. Consider the outcome of their way of life, and imitate their faith" (Heb. 13:7).

To be faithful disciple-makers, we must supply people with imperfect examples of how to love others, demonstrate joy in tough circumstances, pursue peace with neighbors, exhibit patience in trials, express kindness in conflict, embody gentleness when offering correction, and model self-control in all things. We should be like living Bibles who illustrate devotion to Christ.

Do You Have Failures?

Denise had a thousand reasons why God couldn't use her. Her past sins, her present anxieties, and her fear of the future all felt like too much to overcome. She didn't pray enough, didn't know the Bible enough, and wasn't smart enough to answer questions. But one day a godly woman in the church helped her realize that her weakness was actually an opportunity for God to work. Together, they meditated on Jesus's words to

Paul in 2 Corinthians 12:9, "My grace is sufficient for you, for my power is made perfect in weakness." Discipling others involves serving them from the grace God has given you. Have you drawn from the well of God's grace in times of weakness, affliction, and failure? Then serve others with that grace and allow them to be blessed by it as well (2 Cor. 1:3–11).

To be clear, seasons of sinful compromises can hinder our usefulness. Paul assured Timothy that personal holiness makes us useful to the Lord, whereas hypocrisy hinders us and grieves God (Eph. 4:30). If you are struggling with an abiding sin or if you're in a uniquely trying season, speak candidly with one of your pastors about whether you're in a healthy place to invest in others. If you need to step away from discipling work to grow for a season, just remember the Lord wastes nothing and can restore the time we've lost (Joel 2:25–26).

Whom Should I Disciple?

Finding someone to disciple isn't complicated, but it does require wisdom. We each have limited time and energy, so we need to discern how to focus our discipling efforts (Gal. 6:10). And since we need wisdom, the first thing we should do is pray and ask for it (James 1:5). Ask God to show you whom to disciple. Jesus won't send you an email with a list of names to pursue, but his Spirit will guide you. Discipling others is in accordance with his will, and God promises to hear prayers like these (1 John 5:14).

After prayer, let me offer several principles to help you know how to prioritize discipling relationships.

Family

Gospel responsibilities begin with those closest to home. Paul told Timothy, "If anyone does not provide for his relatives, and especially for members of his household, he has denied the faith and is worse than an unbeliever" (1 Tim. 5:8). If this is true of physical needs, how much more spiritual needs? God commands parents to raise their children "in the discipline and instruction of the Lord" (Eph. 6:4) and to see every waking hour as an opportunity for discipling conversations (Deut. 6:7). Likewise, husbands and wives have the responsibility to do intentional spiritual good to one another (Prov. 31:12; Eph. 5:25–26).

Since each family is unique, discipling at home will look different. Some families might have intentional, planned times for Scripture reading, prayer, and spiritual conversations. Others might choose to simply weave biblical encouragement into conversation throughout the day. Whatever the case, husbands and wives should have a plan for how they intend to do spiritual good to each other and to their children.

Fellow Church Members

The local church is a discipling greenhouse. It's where fellow believers gather to hear God's word and sing God's praises. If you're looking to disciple others, then I'm assuming you regularly attend your local church, you're active in serving its needs, you're practicing hospitality, you're applying the gospel to others, and you're loving others as Christ has loved you (John 13:34–35). When we gather with our church family, we should prayerfully look for fellow church members we could invest in.

Who might that be?

Well, don't look for people who have it all together; you won't find any. Look for FAT disciples, that is, disciples who have *Faith*, are *Available*, and are *Teachable*.

Faith. First and foremost, the person you're seeking to disciple must have faith. If someone doesn't have faith, you shouldn't enter into a discipling relationship with that person. You should enter into an evangelistic one. Someone can't obey Jesus's commands if he or she doesn't embrace Jesus's work on the cross and his empty tomb. An unbelieving heart can't obey God (Rom. 8:7). Evangelism, therefore, is the first part of the disciple-making process—one we can't bypass.

Available. Hungry people make time to eat. That obvious fact is true physically and spiritually. Find someone who is eager to grow spiritually and willing to make time for spiritual conversation. Luke's Gospel warns us not to be like Martha who was so busy that she couldn't stop to sit at the feet of Jesus (Luke 10:38–42).

How Do I Disciple Others?

Is the person you're considering willing to make time to grow? Does he faithfully attend corporate worship? Is she disciplining herself to pray, study, and spend time with others? Also, look for those who are already seeking you out. Who lingers for more conversation after your small group is over? Who consistently shows up to the Sunday school class you're attending? Who already seeks you or your family out for counsel?

Teachable. Humble people are willing to do whatever it takes to grow. Katherine came to Christ later in life. She'd been through a painful divorce and was drained from both her suffering under the cruelty of others and the sin done *by* her. But from the moment she began attending our church, she was eager to grow. She came to any study she could, prayed for everyone she met, and asked lots of great questions. She humbly opened herself to correction. Teachable people willingly receive instruction from God's word, desire to have blind spots exposed, and accept correction when wrong. Watch for people like Katherine and fan their flames into a fire.

The best folks to pour energy into are faithful, available, and teachable. But remember, they're not perfect. In fact, let me offer a few quick words of caution.

First, don't overlook the unimpressive. We should judge "no one according to the flesh" (2 Cor. 5:16). After all, not many of us are wise or powerful or noble "according to worldly standards" (1 Cor. 1:26). Don't look for discipling candidates as if you're judging a beauty pageant or picking a sports team at recess (Prov. 31:30). Remember, Jesus's twelve had plenty of flaws and failures. Just because someone is weak, tempted, bereaved, or otherwise "unimpressive" doesn't mean he or she is unworthy of your time. Prayerfully seek humble, hungry people to invest in.

Second, give screw-ups second (and third and fourth) chances. John Mark accompanied Paul and Barnabas on an early missionary journey. Somewhere along the way, he defected from the ministry. We don't know all the details, but whatever happened was enough to convince Paul that Mark was untrustworthy, which eventually led to a split between him and Barnabas (Acts 15:36–41). It would have been easy to write off John Mark after his public failure. But God wasn't done with him, and neither were some in the church.

Barnabas continued investing in John Mark, as did Peter, who worked with Mark to write his Gospel. Peter later mentioned Mark in a letter written roughly twelve years after Mark's failure (1 Pet. 5:13). At the end of Paul's life, while he awaited execution, he wrote to Timothy and told him to "get Mark and bring him with you, for he is very useful to me for ministry" (2 Tim. 4:11). God had used the discipling efforts of some in the church to bring healing, growth, and restoration.

Some immature believers will have patterns of sinful compromise that could tempt you to write them off. Be slow to dismiss them because they've made serious or repeated compromises with sin. Remember, those who have been forgiven much love much (Luke 7:47). God can change the most passionate compromisers into deeply dedicated followers.

Third, consider gender carefully. Just as in a family, brothers and sisters in the local church benefit from one another spiritually. We find this pattern throughout Scripture. Jesus instructed Mary while she sat at his feet (Luke 10:38–42). Lydia hosted and ministered to Paul (Acts 16:14–15). Priscilla and Aquila corrected Apollos (18:24–28). The church has always been filled with men and women who edify one another.

At the same time, recognize that discipling relationships often create deep and intimate spiritual bonds between people. Sharing scriptural insights and heart-felt prayer requests cultivates spiritual affection. Members of the opposite sex can easily become emotionally entangled in ways that distract from the goal of discipling. If attraction grows, it could lead to hurt, a preoccupation with romantic feelings, or even sinful compromise. While we should love and build up both our brothers and sisters in the church, we should also labor to avoid confusing relationships. Thus, it's wise to follow the scriptural pattern of cultivating discipling relationships only with someone of the same gender as yourself. This pattern is clearly portrayed in Scripture in passages like 2 Timothy 2:1–2 and Titus 2:3–5. Also Jesus chose twelve men to be his closest disciples, and Paul partnered primarily with men like Barnabas, Timothy, Titus, Silas, and Luke.

Fourth, intentionally diversify your relationships. Some of my richest discipling relationships have been with people who were different from me. Daniel was a young believer who began attending our church in the early days of my pastorate. We came from different cultural and ethnic backgrounds. He'd been through health and family challenges I hadn't. I had my own share of joys and sorrows that were foreign to him. Our differences were challenging at times, but in God's perfect wisdom, God used these differences to forge a deeper love than could have been possible otherwise. In many ways, I discipled him; in other ways, he discipled me. He's helped me consider interpretations and applications of God's word that I may never have had apart from him.

Diversity in discipling enhances our ability to behold the glory of Jesus. When we encounter members of his body who look different than us, think differently from us, vote differently from us, and experience life differently than we do, we are encouraged in unique ways. I want to challenge you to seek out discipling relationships with the people who are different from you. God will use your differences to teach both of you to love in meaningful ways. The kingdom of God is made of people from every tribe, language, and nation (Rev. 7:9). As much as possible, our discipling relationships should be as well.

You may live in an area without much ethnic diversity, but your church likely has folks from different cultural backgrounds, economic situations, and political affiliations. Every local church has old and young, married and single, simple and sophisticated—all bowing before Jesus. The more time you spend with people who experience life differently than you do, the more you will see the grace of God shine through them in compelling ways. Ask God to give you humility as he uses your differences to shape you both into the image of Jesus.

How to Disciple: Practices

Discipling relationships are an ecosystem of spiritual growth. There are a variety of factors that contribute to the health and growth of a disciple. What follows are ten of the most vital elements of any discipling relationship.

1. Prayer

Brian was a fellow pastor who challenged me toward Christlikeness in many ways—particularly in prayer. He regularly ended our conversations by saying, "Let's pray about that," and then interceded on my behalf. To this day, I'm helped by Brian's example.

Brian was simply modeling his own ministry after Jesus. Jesus prayed for and with his disciples (John 11:41–42; 17). He taught them how to pray and challenged them to remain vigilant in prayer (Matt. 26:41; Luke 11:1–13).

Pray regularly for and with the people you're discipling. Let them know that you're praying for them. As they navigate daily life, remind them to take their needs to the throne of grace (Heb. 4:14–16). Consider reading books on prayer, regularly sharing prayer requests, and carving out time to pray together.

Discipling without prayer is like running without breathing. When a discipling relationship is marked by constantly looking to Jesus in prayer together, you'll find unique help.

2. Go to Church Together

The local church is central to the mission of making disciples. It's not only where we can find people to disciple, it's also where the most important discipling in the Christian life occurs. In the local church, we all gather to hear God's word prayed, read, preached, and applied. It's where we sing God's word to one another and see God's word in the ordinances. Take what you received from the service and process with those you're discipling over a meal, text message, or phone call. While you don't have to sit with each other during Sunday gatherings, what happens during the gathering supplies endless fodder for discipling conversations.

3. Be Equipped by Pastors

As you invest in the lives of others, ask your pastors to invest in you. Even if you're an experienced discipler, sitting down with one of your pastors and reviewing your discipling efforts will likely be edifying. Part of your pastor's job description is to equip you for the work of the ministry (Eph. 4:11–12). So ask a pastor to counsel you on whom you're discipling, how you're discipling, and how you can grow. As you encounter difficult subjects, questions, or concerns, ask a pastor to help you. Pastors have no greater joy than assisting in this type of request.

4. Saturate Everything with Scripture

The people who have most impacted my life for Jesus have been those who saturate everything they say with God's word. One of my first mentors was Tommy. I was new in the faith and had many questions, so a friend and I took Tommy out for breakfast. We had written down roughly two dozen questions, and we wanted him to help us. To our amazement, he answered each question by quoting Scripture and then applying it to what we asked. Tommy inspired me to love God's word, trust God's word, and devote my life to helping others do the same.

Teach others to love God's word. Read and study books of the Bible together. As you read

God's word, look for applications and strive to help each other obey them. Bring biblical wisdom to bear on all you say and do. Let Scripture shape your relationships, your money, and your free time. Show them that the Bible "is no empty word for you, but your very life" (Deut. 32:47).

At the end of his life, the apostle Peter challenged the church to pursue Christlikeness by saying, "I intend always to remind you of these qualities, though you know them and are established in the truth that you have. I think it right, as long as I am in this body, to stir you up by way of reminder" (2 Pet.1:12–13). Like Peter, your discipling ministry should be a ministry of reminding—because we are so prone to forget (Deut. 8:11–17). Resist the desire to be overly creative or innovative. We can't do better than simply reminding others of God's word. If you're looking for a good place to start, study the "one another" passages of the New Testament and challenge each other to find fresh ways to apply them. Or ask your pastor to recommend a book that will help you study Scripture together.

5. Open Your Life

The task of discipling can't be reduced to a curriculum. It's an invitation to learn from observing embodied faith. Paul called Corinthian believers to "be imitators of me, as I am of Christ" (1 Cor. 11:1). Jesus modeled everything he taught, even washing his disciples' feet, explaining "I have given you an example, that you also should do just as I have done to you" (John 13:15). Discipling invites imitation.

Bethany approached discipling by inviting sisters to "come and see" her faith in everyday life. She wasn't trying to show off a perfect life—but an authentic one. While chatting over coffee, going to the grocery store, walking in the park while kids played, or working around the house, she had an open-home, open-life philosophy of discipling. Those she invested in heard her pray, watched her handle conflict, and observed her asking for forgiveness.

As you disciple others, *share* lessons from Scripture. But don't forget to *show* them too. Remember the Christian life isn't just taught, it's also caught.

6. Ask Questions

John was a particularly insightful mentor. Like other disciplers in my life, he knew the Scriptures and walked closely with Jesus. But what made John uniquely helpful were his intentional, incisive questions. Proverbs 20:5 says,

> The purpose in a man's heart is like deep water,
> but a man of understanding will draw it out.

John's thoughtful questions had a way of drawing out the idols, emotions, and unseen issues of my heart. As a result, his counsel always fit the unique needs of my soul in any given moment (Eph. 4:29).

Use questions to help others explore how they relate to Jesus as Lord over every area of their lives.

- *Relationships.* Do you have any relationships where you've cultivated coldness, bitterness, or unforgiveness? To whom are you tempted to show favoritism? Are there any tough conversations you need to have? Whom could you encourage today?

How Do I Disciple Others?

- *Money.* If your bank and credit card statements are theological statements that reveal what you love and trust in, what do your spending, saving, and sharing habits reveal about you? Are you generous or greedy? Do you owe anyone money? How are you handling stress associated with money? What do these stresses reveal about you?
- *Sex.* Are you honoring the Lord with what you look at online? If you are unmarried, are you pursuing relationships with people you are interested in? If so, are you acting honorably? If you are married, are you treating your spouse with tenderness, kindness, and sacrificial love? How are areas of conflict, intimacy, and encouragement going?
- *Time.* Time is life's most invaluable limited resource. How are you using it? Are you redeeming the time and aiming to live wisely in light of eternity (Ps. 90:12; Eph. 5:15–17)? What are you reading, watching, and listening to? Are you retreating too much to the world for entertainment? Is your entertainment helping you to love and appreciate God, or is it callousing you toward things that grieve God?

7. Develop Spiritual Disciplines

Obedience in the Christian life isn't optional (Heb. 12:14). In order to foster a life of holy obedience we need to cultivate spiritual discipline. Therefore an important part of discipling is teaching others how to train themselves for godliness (1 Tim. 4:7).

Discipline isn't an end in itself but a means to producing Christlikeness. We read Scripture, pray, fast, sing, confess sins, and engage in other disciplines to know, love, and please God. As we do these things, we'll be better equipped to serve our local church when it gathers to engage in the disciplines of hearing sermons, singing, serving, giving, and observing the ordinances. Discipling must include helping fellow believers to grow in spiritual disciplines so that they and their church body will grow into maturity (Eph. 4:12–16).

8. Encourage Progress

Encouragement is oil in the church's engine. If absent, people will become disheartened and lose motivation to persevere. Our discipling must "consider how to stir up one another to love and good works . . . encouraging one another, and all the more as you see the Day drawing near" (Heb. 10:24–25). So if you see something, say something. Send a text or make a call to point out evidences of God's grace that you see in the people you're discipling. Did they resist temptation? Celebrate with them. Do you see progress in their lives? Point it out. Encouragement inspires obedience and provokes perseverance, so give encouragement generously.

9. Engage with Unbelievers

Discipling should include evangelism. Like Jesus, we must help people become fishers of men (Matt. 4:19). A casual reading of the New Testament shows that Christ expects all believers to be actively engaged in proclaiming the gospel to the lost. Hopefully, evangelism is already a natural part of your life. As you spend time with those you disciple, they should see you engage with unbelievers. You may also invite those you disciple to join you for neighborhood evangelism or in putting on a barbecue for unbelieving friends or coworkers.

I try to encourage others to notice who God has put in their everyday area of influence and to prayerfully seek gospel opportunities. I also regularly pray for opportunities to engage the lost. Here are four prayers I challenge others to pray.

1. "God, help me see lost people as you do." Ask God to enlighten the eyes of your heart to see people from an eternal perspective (2 Cor. 5:16; Matt. 25:46).
2. "God, open doors for the gospel." Ask God to arrange divine opportunities to proclaim the gospel as well as attentiveness to recognize them (Col. 4:2–3).
3. "God, give me courage to proclaim Jesus." Jesus assured us that his presence would accompany us, so asking for boldness is in line with his will (Matt. 28:18–20; Eph. 6:19–20).
4. "God, let me see conversions." Plead with God together, asking him to remove the veil of unbelief from unbelievers' eyes so they can see Christ's glory and be saved (2 Cor. 4:4).

As you evangelize together, remind one another to draw strength from the gospel you are proclaiming. Remind each other that you need God's grace to proclaim God's grace. And never forget that Jesus assures us he will be with us as our help every step of the way (Matt. 28:20).

10. Teach Disciples to Suffer

Suffering is inevitable for disciples of Jesus. If we follow him, we will encounter suffering just as he did (Matt. 10:16–25). The apostle Peter affirmed this reality, "Beloved, do not be surprised at the fiery trial when it comes upon you to test you, as though something strange were happening to you" (1 Pet. 4:12).

Suffering is certain, so we must prepare those we disciple for it. Study passages about persecution, affliction, death, difficult providences, and consider their implications.[3] When we endure suffering, we allow those we invest in to weep with us as we wrestle with the Lord. While we reserve the right to privacy in hard times, we must not forget that God gives us grace in our affliction so we can give it to others in theirs (2 Cor. 1:3–11).

Ben and Anna moved into our family's home as young Christians. My wife and I invested in them for several years, and we saw them flourish in Christ. As they prepared to plant a church, they discovered they were pregnant with a baby boy. Their rejoicing, however, soon turned to reeling when their son received a fatal diagnosis. They were blessed to have John Joseph Robin for seventeen days before they laid him to rest. Few things are more heart-wrenching than burying a child. And yet, through their grief, they invited others to weep with them, and though they didn't realize it, to learn how to trust God in darkness. Ben and Anna showed me how to walk with God in the valley of death. While grieving himself, Ben loved his grieving wife, and Anna honestly lamented in ways that deeply impacted us. Through their suffering, the friends we discipled became the ones discipling us.

How to Disciple: Posture

Discipling isn't just about what we do, but also how we do it. If we aren't careful, we can become overly programmatic in our approach to discipling, and our relationships can become robotic. What follows are seven heart postures I'd urge you to cultivate in your discipling relationships.

1. Disciple Prayerfully

Why bring up prayer again? Because it's so easily neglected! Discipling requires divine intervention. Helping others become like Jesus is a hopeless endeavor unless God empowers our labors (Ps. 127:1). Follow Paul's example who told Timothy, "I thank God whom I serve . . . as I remember you constantly in my prayers night and day" (2 Tim. 1:3). Ask God to give you wisdom as you disciple others. Pray before you spend time with them, while you're with them, and afterward.

2. Disciple Intentionally

Discipling won't just happen. It requires you to pray, plan, and pursue others with intentionality. Even Jesus's ministry demonstrates focused, intentional investment. He called his followers to become "fishers of men" (Matt. 4:19). Everything he taught and did had this mission in mind. He was preparing them to take the baton of gospel ministry to the nations after his ascension (Matt. 28:18–20).

As you invest in others, ensure that you read, study, pray, encourage, and correct with knowing Jesus and making him known as the main aim. Also, be intentional with passing out opportunities to lead. Allow others to lead your meeting by deciding what to discuss, preparing the lesson, or picking what questions, topics, or passages to work through. In this sense, allow your times together to be a two-way street.

3. Disciple Dependently

Discipling requires us to embrace a mysterious paradox: we serve in God's strength (1 Cor. 15:10; Phil. 2:12–13; 4:13; 1 Pet. 4:11). We labor for Jesus by depending on the one who tells us, "Apart from me you can do nothing" (John 15:5).

But how do we serve in God's strength?

If you're in a rowboat, any hope of progress comes from your efforts. But that's not the case with sailing. For a sailboat to move, you must raise the sail. Doing this requires faith-filled effort. You pull the halyard, believing that as you raise the sail, it will harness the power of the wind and push you along. In the same way, we raise the divine-strength-harnessing-sail through prayer together, by obeying commands and confessing sins together, by enduring suffering together, and by countless other acts of faith. As we do, the strength of God's Spirit empowers our efforts and bears fruit. Dependence on God gives him the glory he deserves and us the strength we need.

4. Disciple Creatively

Jesus's discipling was dynamic. Every circumstance provided a creative possibility for applying God's truth. He gave lessons on a hillside (Matthew 5–7), in a vineyard (John 15), and at funerals (John 11). He taught his disciples in the synagogue (Mark 6:1–6), while fishing (Luke 5:1–11), and over meals (Luke 7:36–50). Jesus pointed out positive and negative examples from the people they encountered (Matthew 23; Mark 12:41–44). Discipling isn't limited to reading the Bible for an hour over coffee once a week. Take walks in nature, visit nursing homes, go shopping, or host a barbecue for unbelieving neighbors. The possibilities for connecting Scripture to the world around you are unlimited and will keep your discipling applications fresh.

5. Disciple Urgently

We're not promised tomorrow, so we should help people follow Jesus with urgency. The harvest is plentiful (Matt. 9:37–38), Satan is prowling (1 Pet. 5:8), and Christ may return at any moment (Matt. 24:36–51). Therefore, we must "number our days" and "redeem the time" (Ps. 90:12; Eph. 5:14–17). Remind those you're discipling that we should never delay obedience to God (James 4:17).

6. Disciple Patiently

Disciple urgently, but harness your urgency with patience. People change slowly. God often uses a crockpot not a microwave. As you invest in others, remember that "love is patient" (1 Cor. 13:4). Jesus often used the illustration of farming to describe how spiritual growth happens in his kingdom (Mark 4:26–29). Growing mature Christians, like growing crops, takes time. So don't give up on people if they slowly progress from one degree of glory to another (2 Cor. 3:18). Renewing the mind is a lifelong process (Rom. 12:1–2). And when you're tempted toward impatience, remember how patient God has been with you.

7. Disciple Hopefully

Discipling can be discouraging. We may feel like we aren't making a difference and the people we're investing in aren't making progress. Criticism can blindside us. Apathy can overtake us. But we must allow God's promise to inspire us, "He who began a good work in you will bring it to completion at the day of Jesus Christ" (Phil. 1:6). Remember: the power that raised Jesus from the dead is at work in them—and in you (Eph. 1:19–21). No sin is too strong, no depression is too deep, no addiction is too oppressive, and no trauma is too terrible that God cannot deliver (Isa. 59:1). Do not lose hope. God is always working in our lives and the lives of others—even when it's tough to spot.

Pitfalls to Avoid

As you get going doing spiritual good to others, consider a couple of pitfalls you should avoid. The following list isn't exhaustive, but hopefully it will help you approach the discipling task with wisdom.

1. Don't Be Possessive

Well-meaning people can be tempted to approach discipling with an unhealthy possessiveness. I've been in ministry circles where people call those they invest in "my disciples." They become strangely jealous when others give advice to "their disciples." Let's not get things twisted: they are not *your* disciples. They are Jesus's disciples. He bought them with his blood. He calls you to help them follow him—and to invite others to do the same.

Discipling is designed as partnership with God and other believers. Paul reminded the Corinthians, "I planted, Apollos watered, but God gave the growth. So neither he who plants nor he who waters is anything, but only God who gives the growth" (1 Cor. 3:6–7). No one person is sufficient to completely disciple another person. We best serve others by pointing them to other faithful Christians who can help them as well. Don't make disciples codependent on you and don't be codependent on them. All discipling should foster dependence on Jesus.

2. Don't Circumvent the Local Church

As a young believer, I took part in several parachurch ministries. I was blessed by them, but they often undervalued the local church. Their emphasis on the universal church short-circuited God's plan to shape and mature believers in local churches. Worship meetings, service opportunities, and community fellowship was typically segregated from the church.

The normative New Testament pattern for spiritual growth is in the committed membership of a local church under the oversight of godly elders. In that context, disciples are built up by people from all walks and stages of life. Parachurch ministries, though helpful, lack the biblical authority and design to help believers grow best. In your zeal to disciple others, make sure that you point them toward the local church, not away from it.

3. Don't Fear People

Proverbs 29:25 warns us,

> The fear of man lays a snare,
>   but whoever trusts in the LORD is safe.

Fear of man is dangerous in every arena of life, including discipling. If you fear people, you will not love them well. Fear can hinder you from sharing your struggles or weaknesses because you want to impress them. Fear might keep you from asking penetrating questions or calling out sin. Don't let fear of others (or fear of losing what they can do for you) lead you down a path that could hinder someone's eternal destiny.

4. Don't Be Rigid

Life is messy, so discipling requires flexibility. If your discipling plan can't adapt to what's going on in a person's life, you may unintentionally undermine the gospel truths you proclaim.

I learned this principle the hard way. Early in my walk with the Lord, I was zealous about discipling. I often met with younger brothers to study books of the Bible. I was so committed to my plans that, at times, I lost sight of the people in front of me.

I won't forget the time a young man sat at my kitchen table and shared his doubts about the Lord and struggles with sin that were consuming his life. I prayed for him and then instead of detouring from my discipling plan to walk with him through his trial, we pressed on through the lesson I had planned. My rigidity hindered love and confused him even more about God. It's good to be focused, but you must also be flexible.

5. Don't Hold Yourself Responsible for the Sins of Others

We are responsible for how we minister to others, but not how they respond. People will sin, even when you warn them not to. Some will fall away despite your pleading. Some might betray you, despite of your love for them. Jesus had his Judas, Paul his Demas, and you will have them too. Do not allow others' sins to shackle you with guilt. Their sin is not your fault. In the end, we are each responsible for how we respond to God. He alone can bear their sins. You may weep over their sins, but do "not grow weary in doing good" (Gal. 6:9).

6. Don't Be a Hypocrite

Jesus assured us, "A disciple is not above his teacher, but everyone when he is fully trained will be like his teacher" (Luke 6:40). He goes on to warn that this sort of hypocrisy will be deadly for those trained by it (vv. 41–49). Beware of being harder on others than you are on yourself. If you instruct others, make sure you instruct yourself so that God's name will not be blasphemed (Rom. 2:21–24). One of the best ways to combat hypocrisy is by ensuring that you too are being discipled. We never graduate from the need to be invested in by other faithful believers. All of the pastors I serve with are in some sort of mutually edifying relationship with other believers who help them pursue humility, holiness, and happiness in Christ. No matter your maturity, remain teachable and accountable.

7. Don't Ignore Your Limitations

John the Baptist was clear with his followers: "I am not the Christ" (John 1:20). He knew his limitations. So must we. Our discipling ability and availability will change throughout our lives. In some seasons we'll be able to invest more time and effort in discipling. Other seasons might be less active. We can't be everywhere for everyone. Instead, we must strive to be faithful in the work God sets before us.

You can't fix everything for everyone, and you shouldn't try. Some things will simply be out of your control. You shouldn't feel like you have to have all the answers. After all, the best discipling involves helping people lean on God, who knows what we don't know.[4] So enjoy the liberty that comes with recognizing that God cares for people in all the ways we cannot. Recognizing his all-sufficiency won't create apathy, it'll create deep humility as you point others to him.

When Discipling Is Done

John Bunyan's *Pilgrim's Progress* is an allegory of the Christian life. The main character (appropriately named Christian) travels from the City of Destruction to the Celestial City. Many trials, temptations, and tribulations attempt to deter his progress. But Christian perseveres largely on account of his traveling companions. God providentially provides friends in just the right seasons for just the right reasons. *Help* swoops in to save him from the Slough of Despond. *Interpreter* teaches Christian to see with spiritual eyes. *Faithful* suffers with him in the crucible of Vanity Fair. *Hopeful* holds Christian back from succumbing to suicide. The saints at Palace Beautiful exhort Christian to keep pressing on. Even in Christian's dying moments, *Hopeful* helps him cling to God's promises.[5]

Disciplers have the honor of helping fellow pilgrims finish their race of faith. As we go about that work, we must keep our gaze on Zion's shores. An eternal perspective strengthens the steps of pilgrim perseverance. It keeps obstacles and afflictions in their proper perspective. So speak often of Christ's return. Help others pursue purity today in light of the final day (1 John 2:28–3:3). Set their hearts on the day when suffering will be eclipsed by glory (Rom. 8:18). Assure them that once they enter their eternal home, it will be well worth whatever it cost them. Assure them of this truth: ten thousand years from now, when we know what God knows, we will not accuse him of any wrongdoing.

He has always been faithful. So keep an eternal perspective in your discipling. We're almost home.

Recommended Resource

Mark Dever, *Discipling: How to Help Others Follow Jesus* (Wheaton, IL: Crossway, 2016)

Notes

1. Some content in these first two sections is drawn from my other Church Questions booklet *How Can I Find Someone to Disciple Me?* (Wheaton, IL: Crossway, 2021).
2. When possible, personal stories in this booklet are shared with permission from those involved, and some names have been changed for privacy.
3. Consider Joseph's life (Genesis 37–50), the book of Job, the Psalms of Lament (see for instance Psalms 6, 13, 22, 42, 60, and 88), the Gospels, Romans 8, the book of 1 Peter, and the book of Revelation.
4. Hat-tip to Zach Eswine's wonderful book *The Imperfect Pastor: Discovering Joy in Our Limitations through a Daily Apprenticeship with Jesus* (Wheaton, IL: Crossway, 2015) for these invaluable lessons.
5. I've quoted here from my article on the importance of John Bunyan in my life in "The Pastor's Progress: Why I Keep Reading John Bunyan," desiring God, January 3, 2023, https://www.desiringgod.org.

Scripture Index

Deuteronomy
6:7 20–21
8:11–17 32
32:47 32

Psalms
90:12 .... 35, 44
127:1 41

Proverbs
20:5 34
29:25 48
31:12 21
31:30 24

Isaiah
59:1 45

Joel
2:25–26 19

Matthew
4:19 .... 17, 37, 41
5–7 43
9:37–38 44
10:16–25 39
23 43
23:15 17
24:36–51 44
25:46 38
26:41 29
28:18–20 .... 12, 14, 38, 42
28:19 10
28:20 .... 13, 14, 39

Mark
4:26–29 44–45
6:1–6 43
12:41–44 43

Scripture Index

Luke
5:1–11	43
6:40	50
6:41–49	50
7:36–50	43
7:47	25
9:23–26	11
10:38–42	22, 26
11:1–13	29

John
1:20	51
1:46	10
11	43
11:41–42	29
13:15	33
13:34–35	15, 21
15	43
15:5	14, 42
15:11	14
17	29
17:23	15

Acts
1:8	14
15:36–41	24
16:14–15	26
18:24–28	26

Romans
1:11–12	16
2:21–24	50
8:7	22
8:18	52–53
12:1–2	45

1 Corinthians
1:26	24
3:6–7	46
11:1	17, 33
13:4	44
15:10	42

2 Corinthians
1:3–11	19, 39
3:18	45
4:4	38
5:9	13
5:16	24, 38
12:9	19

Galatians
6:9	50
6:10	20

Ephesians
1:19–21	45
4:11–12	31
4:12–16	14, 36
4:29	34
4:30	19
5:10	13
5:14–17	44
5:15–17	35
5:25–26	21

Scripture Index

6:4 20
6:19–20 38

Philippians
1:6 45
2:12–13 42
4:13 42

Colossians
1:10 13
4:2–3 38

1 Thessalonians
5:11 14

1 Timothy
4:7 36
5:8 20

2 Timothy
1:3 41
2:1–2 26
4:11 25

Titus
2:3–5 26

Hebrews
4:14–16 29
10:24–25 37
12:14 36
13:7 18

James
1:5 20
4:17 44

1 Peter
2:21 11
4:11 42
4:12 39
5:8 44
5:13 25

2 Peter
1:12–13 32

1 John
2:28–3:3 52
3:22 13
5:14 20

Revelation
7:9 28

Building Healthy Churches

9Marks exists to equip church leaders with a biblical vision and practical resources for displaying God's glory to the nations through healthy churches.

To that end, we want to see churches characterized by these nine marks of health:

1. Expositional Preaching
2. Gospel Doctrine
3. A Biblical Understanding of Conversion and Evangelism
4. Biblical Church Membership
5. Biblical Church Discipline
6. A Biblical Concern for Discipleship and Growth
7. Biblical Church Leadership
8. A Biblical Understanding of the Practice of Prayer
9. A Biblical Understanding and Practice of Missions

Find all our Crossway titles and other resources at 9Marks.org.

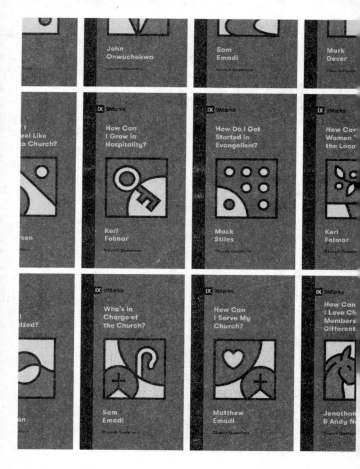

IX 9Marks Church Questions

Providing ordinary Christians with sound and accessible biblical teaching by answering common questions about church life.

For more information, visit crossway.org.